Low Fat Cuisine

© Honos Verlag GmbH, a subsidiary of
VEMAG Verlags- und Medien Aktiengesellschaft, Cologne
www.apollo-intermedia.de

Complete production: Honos Verlag GmbH, Cologne
Printed in China

ISBN 3–8299–0836–9

Low Fat Cuisine

HONOS
VERLAG

CONTENTS

Low-fat cuisine 6

Appetizers and snacks 12

Soups and stews................................26

Vegetarian dishes.................................40

Poultry dishes.................................56

Fish and seafood 74

Meat and game dishes..................92

Desserts and puddings 108

Index of recipes.................................120

LOW-FAT CUISINE

Low-fat cuisine is the simple way to the health and weight you desire. Our delicious recipes will make it easy for you to be more conscious of how what you eat, without giving up a thing in terms of flavour!

Fit rather than fat

Proper, healthy nutrition begins in your head rather than in your stomach. Forget everything you have heard about the flash-zoom-bang diets. Ban the images of extra-slim super-models or muscular beach boys from your mind. Think a bit further: the only thing that really matters is feeling your best. Do you manage to strike a good balance, and eat in moderation? If you "swallow" those diet plans the wrong way you may do away not only with the fat, but also with the nutrients in your diet. And this does nothing to enhance your well-being or make you feel your best. The results: frustration and a bad mood, and before you know it you'll be reaching for that candy bar, or beer and potato chips when you come home from work. The vicious circle continues...

It is finally time for you to get back into shape by banishing all those little pads and rolls of fat. You don't have to tolerate a baroque figure! Instead, decide to eat a bit more consciously and pay attention to some basic rules of nutrition. Will power is most certainly part of it! Let's be honest: how often do you choose the greasy fried chips over a mixed salad? Do you order that juicy steak rather than fresh fish when you visit a restaurant? And sports: is that a phenomenon you would rather watch on television?

The decision lies entirely in your hands—but in order to gain control over your body and feel positive about it, you must become more active. Your personal dream figure is not something you can order and you certainly will not achieve it within a fortnight. Instead, achieving that stature is associated with a process that leads slowly but surely to the size you choose to be.

Ground rule number one is **exercise**. An eight-hour office job, escalators, lifts and sitting in front of the television every night—all these things weaken you. As a result, your body runs only at a low level and stores rather than burns newly added fat calories in your bum, stomach and hips. Excess weight is the sure result if you allow this process to run its course without becoming active. On the other hand, it takes only a minimal amount of regular exercise to start burning fat and begin your fight against fat: whenever you can, ride a bicycle instead of driving your car, choose stairs over a comfortable lift ride and go for a walk on a regular basis. And once you start enjoying all this activity you should try jogging, cycling or swimming. Thirty minutes of exercise can work wonders. You will be amazed how quickly even moderate exercise affects your well-being.

Ground rule number two is **balanced and healthy nutrition**. Foods like vegetables, potatoes, rice, pasta and bread deliver complex carbohydrates in the form of starch and leave you feeling satiated. They provide energy in an ideal form for our physical activities and specific bodily functions. About 60 per cent of the daily fuel intake that we offer our body should be in the form of complex carbohydrates. However, it is often the case that fat, instead of carbohydrates, becomes our main source of energy. Therefore, you should pay attention to what is on your plate: include more nutrient-rich complex carbohydrates and reduce fats.

Fibre furthers your health

Not only the quantity of carbohydrates must be right, the quality has to be right as well. It is important to know the difference between simple and complex sugars. The first group includes glucose, fructose and lactose as well as white sugar which is used in the industrial processing of all manner of sweets and sodas. These simple sugars elevate your blood sugar level very quickly, but this level falls just as quickly when the sugar has been used. At that point you again become ravenous, often for something sweet. This is not the case with complex sugars: because of their multiple components, this type of sugar provides energy over a longer period of time, leaving you feel satiated longer!

Try to reduce your intake of sweets and drinks that contain a lot of sugar, and concentrate instead on foods containing vitamins, minerals and fibre. Don't think of fibre as ballast—quite the opposite is true: by eating wholegrain products like oats, wholegrain rice, granola, as well as vegetables and fruit, peas and beans, and to some extent nuts, it will be easier to foster healthy nutrition. This is because you will feel satiated for a long time and your intestines will work more efficiently.

Getting through the day without fat

It is not really difficult to have a healthy diet. Unfortunately we eat much too much: too much fat, too much sugar and too much salt. Even that icon of fast food, the Big Mac, and other similar meals could be made a bit healthier if we wanted them to be.

In addition to the quality of the food we eat, when and how much we eat are also significant factors. Do everything in your power to avoid ravenous hunger, which leads you to devour huge portions that are too much for your metabolism. Try to get used to eating several small meals throughout the day, so that you feel full all day long, and that big wave of hunger will not appear in the first place. In addition to a balanced breakfast and lunch, we recommend a second light breakfast of fruit, yoghurt and granola, as well as a healthy afternoon snack in the form of kefir, buttermilk or fruit, which can tide you over the afternoon blahs.

Dinner should never be the main meal of the day, but should make up only a quarter of you daily food intake. Unfortunately a different trend exists: dinner is the main meal and is often pushed later and later towards the end of the day. For people who work full days or frequent restaurants this trend is a fact of life that may be difficult to avoid. As a rule, however, try to eat dinner as early as possible, preferably between 5:30 and 6:00 pm, or 7:00 pm at the latest. This is crucial because your body slows down its processing of fatty acids towards evening, and increases its storage of fat. You can avoid increasing your stores of fat by eating an evening meal low in fat and protein, emphasizing instead lots of vegetables and complex carbohydrates.

The recipes in this book, given in quantities to serve 4 people, make it easy for you to design your own light cuisine and are meant to offer you inspiration and enjoyment of a healthy and energetic life.

APPETIZERS
AND SNACKS

Whether they are served at the beginning of a
meal or as a small snack, our suggestions for your
light hunger range from fruity to piquant and
taste delicious any time of day.

SCAMPI COCKTAIL ACAPULCO

*Preparation time: about 20 minutes
(plus marinating and chilling time)
Serves 4*

2 mangos
1 orange
2 tbsp lemon juice
8 shrimp
2 tbsp olive oil
salt
fresh ground pepper
ground paprika
40 g (1.5 oz) sugar
3 egg yolks
mint leaves for garnishing

Minute 1
Peel the mangos and cut the flesh into eighths. Squeeze the orange and catch juice in a bowl. Mix in 1 tbsp of the lemon juice and let the mangos marinate in this mixture for about 1 hour.

Minute 4
Wash and dry the shrimp tails. Heat the oil in a fry pan and sauté the shrimp for about 5 minutes. Add salt, pepper and paprika.

Minute 9
Remove the shrimp from the pan and set aside to cool. Pour the remaining lemon juice and 6 tbsp orange juice into a second bowl.

Minute 11
Whisk the sugar and egg yolks into the juices. Beat the mixture over a double boiler until it becomes a foamy cream. Chill for about 30 minutes.

Minute 16
Pry tails carefully off shrimp. Arrange mango pieces and scampi in glass bowls and cover with the cream. Garnish the shrimp cocktails with mint leaves and serve.

CHANKIN SUSHI

Preparation time: about 25 minutes
Serves 4

100 g (3.5 oz) cooked shrimp
2 tbsp rice wine vinegar
1 tbsp mirin
2 tbsp ginger juice
100 g (3.5 oz) broccoli crowns
250 ml (9 fl oz) light miso broth
100 g (3.5 oz) carrots
1 tbsp sesame oil
4 eggs
1 tsp salt
1 pinch ground ginger
2 tbsp butter
100 g (3.5 oz) cooked sushi rice

Minute 1
Combine the shrimp with the rice wine vinegar, mirin and ginger juice. Wash the broccoli and cook it in miso broth for about 4 minutes. Drain and cut into pieces.

Minute 6
Peel and dice the carrots. Heat the oil in a fry pan and sauté the carrots for about 3 minutes. Whisk the eggs with the salt and ginger.

Minute 10
Heat the butter in a fry pan and make thin omelettes with the egg mixture.

Minute 18
Spread omelettes on a cutting board. Knead together the rice, broccoli crowns, carrots and shrimp and form little balls.

Minute 20
Place balls on the omelettes and form small pockets out of them. Tie together with chives.

SPROUT-MUSHROOM SALAD

Preparation time: about 20 minutes
Serves 4

500 g (17 oz) Chinese mushrooms
3 tbsp sesame oil
ginger powder, dried mustard, ground aniseed
300 g (10 oz) alfalfa sprouts
300 g (10 oz) radicchio
3 tbsp apple vinegar
5 tbsp peanut oil
3 tbsp sweet rice wine
2 tbsp soy sauce

Minute 1
Wash and trim the mushrooms, then cut in pieces. Heat the oil in a fry pan and sauté the mushrooms.

Minute 5
Season with the spices and continue cooking a further 3 minutes.

Minute 10
Take mushrooms from the pan. Wash and drain the sprouts.

Minute 12
Wash and dry the radicchio and cut in strips. Add to mushrooms.

Minute 15
Combine the vinegar, peanut oil, rice wine and soy sauce. Add ginger, dried mustard and aniseed to taste.

Minute 19
Add the vinegar mixture to the mushrooms, mix and serve.

AVOCADO SALAD

Preparation time: about 20 minutes
Serves 4

200 g (7 oz) blackberries
3 avocados
3 tbsp lemon juice
200 g (7 oz) mushrooms
2 tbsp butter
salt
2 tbsp lemon pepper
150 g (5 oz) cherry tomatoes
4 tbsp grapefruit juice
3 tbsp banana juice
3 tbsp grenadine syrup
3 puréed kiwifruits
6 tbsp pumpkin seed oil
125 ml (4 fl oz) vegetable broth
pepper

Minute 1
Wash and dry the blackberries. Halve the avocados, remove the stones, peel and cut into thin wedges. Drizzle the lemon juice over them.

Minute 6
Clean and trim the mushrooms then cut in half. Heat the butter in a fry pan and sauté the mushrooms. Add salt and the lemon pepper.

Minute 12
Rinse and halve the tomatoes. Add to the mushrooms and let simmer for about 3 minutes. Remove from the pan and let vegetables cool down.

Minute 18
Stir blackberries and avocado wedges carefully into the mixture. Combine juices and syrup with kiwi purée, pumpkin seed oil and vegetable broth. Add salt and pepper to taste. Pour sauce over the salad and serve garnished with kiwifruit slices.

GREEK SALAD

Preparation time: about 20 minutes
Serves 4

6 plum tomatoes
4 red onions
1 lollo rosso
3 tbsp pitted black olives
3 tbsp pitted green olives
5 tbsp red wine vinegar
6 tbsp olive oil
salt & pepper
sugar
1/2 bunch basil
1/2 bunch oregano
300 g (10 oz) feta cheese

Minute 1
Rinse and trim the tomatoes, then cut in slices. Peel and slice the onions as well.

Minute 5
Wash and drain the lettuce and pull into bite-size pieces. Drain and chop the olives. Put all ingredients in one bowl and mix.

Minute 11
Combine the vinegar with oil, and add salt, pepper and sugar to taste. Wash, drain and mince herbs. Whisk the herbs into the salad dressing.

Minute 17
Cube the feta cheese and mix into salad. Drizzle salad with the dressing and garnish with basil and oregano leaves. A loaf of round flat bread accompanies this dish beautifully.

COOKED ARTICHOKES LUCULLUS

Preparation time: about 20 minutes
Serves 4

| 4 artichokes |
| salt |
| lemon juice |
| pepper |
| 6 tbsp white vinegar |
| 1 hard-cooked egg |
| 2 shallots |
| 1 bunch curly parsley |
| 1 tbsp capers |
| 4 tbsp oil |
| 4 tbsp sugar |
| 1/4 bunch lemon balm |
| 80 g (2.75 oz) soft butter |
| 1 tbsp yoghurt |

Minute 1
Wash and drain the artichokes. Cut off the stems. Bring salted water to the boil and add some lemon juice. Let artichokes simmer over low heat for 15–20 minutes. Stir some salt and pepper into the vinegar.

Minute 8
Peel and finely chop the egg. Peel and dice the shallots. Wash, drain and mince the parsley. Drain capers.

Minute 13
Stir all ingredients into the vinegar mixture and mix in the oil. Add salt, pepper and sugar to taste.

Minute 15
Wash and dry the lemon balm, then pull off some leaves. Beat the butter until creamy. Stir in the yoghurt and lemon balm. Add salt, pepper and sugar to taste.

Minute 19
Dress the artichokes with the vinaigrette and lemon butter.

Minute 8

EXOTIC COURGETTE RAGOUT

Preparation time: about 20 minutes
Serves 4

1 piece fresh ginger (2 cm/1 inch)
3 courgettes
4 tbsp sesame oil
200 g (7 oz) currants
1/2 tsp each ground cinnamon,
coriander, cumin and cardamom
600 ml vegetable broth
100 g (3.5 oz) pineapple pieces
(tinned)
2 bananas
3 tbsp mango chutney (ready-made)
3 tbsp cornflour
4 tbsp unsalted pumpkin seeds

Minute 1
Peel and finely chop the ginger. Wash and trim the courgettes, then halve lengthwise and cut in thick slices.

Minute 5
Heat the sesame oil in a saucepan and sauté the courgette and ginger. Add the currants and spices (adjust to taste).

Minute 7
Pour the vegetable broth in the saucepan with the sautéed vegetables and continue to simmer at low heat for about 8 minutes.

Minute 9
Drain the pineapple pieces in a sieve. Peel the bananas and cut in half lengthwise, then slice.

Minute 15
Combine the fruit with the chutney and courgettes. Add the cornflour and heat everything together for about 3 minutes until it thickens.

Minute 18
Roast the pumpkin seeds in a fry pan with no fat. Serve the courgette ragout topped with the pumpkin seeds. Rice goes well with this dish.

HALIBUT COCKTAIL

Preparation time: about 30 minutes
Serves 4

1 tin artichoke hearts
(about 240 g/8 oz)
200 g (7 oz) smoked halibut fillets
1 tbsp capers
1 twig sage
3 tbsp rosé wine
4 tbsp sherry vinegar
salt
fresh ground pepper
4 tbsp olive oil

Minute 1
Drain the artichoke hearts. Cut the halibut fillets in pieces. Combine them in a bowl and mix. Add capers.

Minute 5
Wash, dry and mince the sage. Set aside a few small leaves for the garnish.

Minute 8
In a bowl, whisk together the wine, sherry vinegar, salt, pepper and olive oil. Add the sage.

Minute 12
Arrange artichoke hearts and fish on plates. Pour sauce on top and let sit for about 15 minutes.

Minute 29
Garnish everything with small sage leaves.

Minute 1

Minute 5

Minute 8

Minute 12

CRABS ON THE SHELL

Preparation time: about 30 minutes
Serves 4

4 crabs (750 g/1 lb 10 oz each)
2 stalks chicory
200 g (7 oz) lamb's lettuce
100 g (3.5 oz) rocket salad
lemon juice
12 kumquats
3 tbsp sunflower seed oil
1 tbsp cream
2 tbsp crème fraîche
1/2 bunch each chervil and dill
salt
fresh ground pepper

Minute 1
Cook crabs in boiling water for about 8 minutes. Remove crabs from liquid and drain. Break the claws and legs off the shell by twisting.

Minute 10
Lift the shell on the underside of the tail and twist off. Slide a knife between the shell and the body while holding the shell firmly. Separate crab meat from the body by sliding a sharp knife along the shell's edge and scoop out the meat with a spoon. Wash the shell. Crack open the claws. Separate crab meat from shell. Cut the legs open and pull out the meat.

Minute 20
Wash and trim the chicory, then cut into strips. Wash and dry the salad greens. Drizzle the lemon juice over the salad. Wash and slice the kumquats. Combine the oil, cream and crème fraîche. Wash, drain and mince the herbs and stir into the dip. Salt and pepper to taste. Fill the crab shells with the salad ingredients and serve garnished with the dip.

TEMAKI SUSHI

Preparation time: about 30 minutes
Makes 20 sushi

100 g (3.5 oz) smoked turkey breast
100 g (3.5 oz) honeydew melon
2 tbsp sake
4 tbsp soy sauce
200 g (7 oz) smoked trout fillets
100 g (3.5 oz) pickled ginger
100 g (3.5 oz) diced cucumber
100 g (3.5 oz) diced tomatoes
1 clove garlic
2 tbsp sherry vinegar
sugar
pepper
dried mustard
40 oysters
2 tbsp pepper butter
20 pickled onions from a jar
10 sheets nori
400 g (14 oz) pre-cooked sushi rice
wasabi paste

Minute 1
Cut turkey breast and melon in strips ca. 5 cm/2 in long, but not too thin. Pour over the sake and 3 tbsp soy sauce.

Minute 4
Cut the trout in strips. Finely chop the ginger. Combine with trout.

Minute 6
Combine cucumber and tomatoes in a bowl. Peel the garlic and press it into the same bowl. Drizzle with the vinegar and add sugar and spices to taste.

Minute 10
Wash the oysters. Heat butter and sauté the oysters. Drain the onions and add to pan. Pour in remaining soy sauce.

Minute 18
Cut nori sheets in half and heat in a fry pan with no fat. Place on each sheet a golf-ball sized ball of rice. Spread wasabi paste on top. Layer alternately with turkey breast, fish, vegetables, or oyster filling and roll up into a cone.

MOREL-OLIVE PAN

Preparation time: about 20 minutes
Serves 4

50 g (1.75 oz) dried morels
300 g (10 oz) marinated black olives
4 cloves garlic
6 tbsp olive oil
75 ml (2.5 fl oz) sherry
1 small dried chilli pepper
1 bunch flat parsley
1 tbsp tomato paste

Minute 1
Rinse the morels and let them
soak in water for 1–2 hours.
Drain the olives in a sieve and
remove pits.

Minute 2
Peel and slice the garlic. Drain
the morels, reserving the water in
which they soaked.

Minute 5
Heat the oil in a fry pan and
sauté the morels and garlic.
Add the olives. Continue to sauté
and stir the mixture for about
2 minutes.

Minute 9
Pour in the sherry and 75 ml
(2.5 fl oz) of the water in which
the mushrooms soaked. Add the
chilli pepper. Heat the mixture for
about 5 minutes and let the liquid
evaporate.

Minute 16
Wash and dry the parsley,
coarsely chop it and add to
the morels. Finally, stir in the
tomato paste and remove the
chilli pepper. Deli-style bread
compliments this meal.

SOUPS
AND STEWS

Everything in one pot: many fresh ingredients
can be combined into imaginative soup
creations. These diverse recipes will
pamper you, and at the same time
are quick and easy to prepare.

MOROCCAN SOUP

Preparation time: about 20 minutes
Serves 4

2 envelopes cream of tomato soup
500 g (17 oz) minced mutton
salt
pepper
garlic powder
chilli powder
1 tbsp oil
1 red onion
300 g (10 oz) courgettes
250 g (8.5 oz) white beans (tinned)
100 g (3.5 oz) couscous

Minute 1
Heat the cream of tomato soup in a saucepan. In a bowl, season the mince with salt, pepper, garlic powder and chilli powder and form small balls.

Minute 6
Heat the oil in a fry pan and brown the meatballs for about 5 minutes. Peel and dice the onion and it add to meatballs.

Minute 10
Wash and trim the courgettes. Dice them and add to the pan as well.

Minute 12
Stir the meatballs and vegetables into the tomato soup. Add the beans and couscous and let simmer for about 8 minutes. Season with salt and pepper.

Minute 6

28

CREAM SOUP WITH CRAB MEAT

Preparation time: about 30 minutes
Serves 4

---

500 g (17 oz) sweet potatoes (batata)

150 g (5 oz) carrots

1 onion

100 g (3.5 oz) celery stalks

500 ml (17 fl oz) milk

250 ml (9 fl oz) fish stock

2 bay leaves

1 tbsp sweet paprika

Worcestershire sauce

100 g (3.5 oz) crab meat

fresh chervil to garnish

Minute 1
Wash and peel the batata and cut into cubes. Trim and peel the carrots, then dice.

Minute 6
Peel and chop the onion. Wash and trim the celery stalks then cut into small pieces.

Minute 10
Combine the vegetables, milk and fish stock in a large pot and bring to the boil. Add the bay leaves and paprika and cook over low heat for about 15 minutes.

Minute 25
Take out bay leaves and purée everything. Add Worcestershire sauce to taste.

Minute 27
Heat the crab meat in the soup. When warmed through, ladle soup onto plates and garnish with fresh chervil.

Minute 10

MUSHROOM SOUP WITH PUFF PASTRY TOP

Preparation time: about 30 minutes
Serves 4

500 g (17 oz) mushrooms
5 red onions
1/2 bunch parsley
3 tbsp truffle oil
salt & pepper
2 tbsp green peppercorns
1.5 l (1 quart 13 fl oz) mushroom stock
4 ml (a scant tsp) port
1 tbsp lemon juice
100 g (3.5 oz) sour cream
2 tbsp double cream
200 g (7 oz) puff pastry (frozen)
1 egg yolk, 2 tbsp milk

Minute 1

Clean and chop mushrooms. Peel onions and cut into rings. Wash and dry parsley, then cut into strips. Heat the oil and sauté the mushrooms and onions. Generously salt and pepper. Add the parsley and peppercorns.

Minute 10

Add the stock, port and lemon juice to the pan and let simmer over low heat for about 4 minutes. Then stir sour cream and double cream into the hot but no longer boiling soup. Let soup cool a bit and pour into soup bowls. Preheat oven to 200 °C/390 °F/gas mark 6. Spread puff pastry onto a flour-dusted surface and cut out circles at least 2 cm (3/4 inch) larger than your soup bowls.

Minute 20

Cover each soup bowl with puff pastry. Whisk egg yolk and milk together and brush some onto the pastry. Place bowls in the centre of the oven for ca. 10 minutes until the top is brown and crispy.

TOMATO SOUP

Preparation time: about 25 minutes
Serves 4

12 ripe tomatoes
1 bunch basil
4 cloves garlic
2 onions
6 tbsp walnut oil
250 ml (9 fl oz) tomato juice
125 ml (4 fl oz) Sangrita
1 tsp sugar
salt
pepper
500 ml (17 fl oz) vegetable broth
100 g (3.5 oz) rocket salad
100 g (3.5 oz) minced walnuts
5 tbsp Emmental cheese

Minute 1

Wash and trim the tomatoes.
Score the skins, then dip into
boiling water for a moment, rinse
in cold water and remove the
skins. Cut the tomatoes in half
and then into cubes. Wash and
pat dry the basil before cutting
into strips. Peel and press the
garlic through a garlic press.
Chop onions.

Minute 12

Heat 4 tbsp of the oil in a pot and
sauté the tomatoes, onions, basil
and half of the garlic. Pour in the
tomato juice and Sangrita. Add
the sugar and salt and pepper to
taste.

Minute 16

Stir in the vegetable broth and
let simmer over low heat for 4–5
minutes. In the meantime, wash
and drain the rocket. Mince it
finely. Purée the rocket, walnuts,
the remaining oil and garlic and
the cheese with a handheld
mixer. Add salt and pepper to
taste. Put soup on plates, garnish
with a dab of minced rocket
salad and serve.

KOHLRABI-THYME SOUP

Preparation time: about 20 minutes
Serves 4

4 medium kohlrabi
1 bunch spring onions
3 tbsp herb butter
salt
freshly ground pepper
freshly ground nutmeg
500 ml (17 fl oz) beef stock
1/4 bunch thyme
200 ml (7 fl oz) cream

Minute 1
Clean, peel and trim the kohlrabi. Cut into strips. Wash and trim the spring onions and cut them into rings.

Minute 5
Heat the butter in a pot and sauté the kohlrabi strips and the spring onions. Add salt, pepper and nutmeg.

Minute 10
Pour in the beef stock, bring to the boil and let simmer at a low heat for about 10 minutes. Wash and drain the thyme, then mince it finely.

Minute 19
Stir the cream into the soup and purée everything thoroughly with a handheld mixer. Garnish the soup with thyme and serve.

OKRA-MUSHROOM SOUP

Preparation time: about 20 minutes
Serves 4

250 g (9 oz) rice
salt
400 g (14 oz) shitake mushrooms
200 g (7 oz) leek
1 tbsp butter
500 ml (17 fl oz) vegetable broth
100 ml (3 fl oz) cream
150 g (5 oz) okra (tinned)
freshly ground pepper
1 tbsp lemon juice
2 tbsp ouzo
1 tsp coriander
fresh coriander to garnish

Minute 1
Cook the rice in boiling salted water for about 15 minutes until it is chewy. Briefly rinse the mushrooms, then slice them.

Minute 5
Trim and clean the leek. Cut it into rings. Heat the butter in a pot and sauté the leek rings.

Minute 8
Add the mushroom slices to the pot and stir. Pour in the broth and cream. Drain the okra and add it to soup.

Minute 10
Let everything simmer over low heat for about 10 minutes. Season the soup with the lemon juice, ouzo, coriander and salt and pepper.

Minute 15
Drain the rice and gently blend it into the soup. Spoon the soup onto plates, garnish with fresh coriander and serve.

Minute 8

EGG-FLOWER BROTH WITH CELERY

Preparation time: about 20 minutes
Serves 4

200 g (7 oz) peas (frozen)
2 carrots
200 (7 oz) celery stalks
1 l (1 quart) vegetable broth
(ready-made)
salt
pepper
4–5 tbsp port
6 medium eggs
100 g (3.5 oz) freshly shredded
Parmesan cheese
1/2 bunch basil

Minute 1
Let the peas thaw a bit. Clean and trim the carrots and celery stalks. Dice both vegetables.

Minute 5
Heat the vegetable broth in a pot and add salt, pepper and the port.

Minute 8
Add the vegetables to the pot and let simmer over a low flame for about 8–10 minutes.

Minute 18
Crack the eggs into a bowl and beat them with a whisk. Season

with salt and pepper. Pour the eggs into the hot broth and let stand for about 1 minute. Then stir carefully.

Minute 19
Wash and drain the basil. Cut it into strips. Ladle the soup into bowls and serve garnished with the Parmesan cheese and fresh basil.

PEA SOUP

Preparation time: about 30 minutes
Serves 4

1 kg (2 lb 3 oz) fresh peas
1 onion
1 bunch chervil
20 g (scant 1 oz) butter
750 ml (1 pt 7 fl oz) veal stock
250 g (9 oz) whipping cream
salt
pepper
cayenne
8 nasturtium blossoms

Minute 1
Shell the peas. Peel and dice the onion.

Minute 7
Wash and dab dry the chervil, then pull off the leaves. Heat the butter in a fry pan and sauté the onion.

Minute 8
Add the peas to the onion. Pour in the veal stock. Bring to the boil and simmer over low heat for about 15 minutes. After that, remove the peas with a slotted spoon.

Minute 23
Add a few chervil leaves to the soup and purée everything a handheld mixer.

Minute 26
Stir the cream into the soup and add salt, pepper, and cayenne to taste.

Minute 28
Put the whole peas back into the soup and blend. Serve garnished with the nasturtium blossoms.

Minute 1

Minute 5

Minute 8

Minute 9

TOMATO STEW

Preparation time: about 30 minutes
Serves 4

1 kg (2 lb 3 oz) beefsteak tomatoes
250 g (9 oz) celery stalks
1 carrot
1 bunch spring onions
40 g (1.5 oz) butter
800 ml (1 pt 8 oz) vegetable broth
salt
freshly ground pepper
1/2 bunch basil
1/2 twig rosemary
3 tbsp shredded Parmesan cheese

Minute 1
Wash and score the skin of the tomatoes. Dip them in boiling water, then remove skins. Dice the tomatoes.

Minute 5
Wash, trim and chop the celery stalks. Clean, peel and slice the carrot.

Minute 8
Clean and trim the spring onions. Cut into rings. Heat the butter in a pot and sauté the vegetables for a short time.

Minute 10
Pour on the vegetable broth, add salt and pepper, and simmer at low heat for about 20 minutes.

Minute 12
Wash and shake dry the basil and rosemary. Cut the basil into strips and pull needles of rosemary from the sprig.

Minute 29
Add the herbs to the soup. Sprinkle each plate of soup with Parmesan cheese before serving.

Soups and stews

COLOURFUL NOODLE SOUP

Preparation time: about 30 minutes
Serves 4

1 l (1 quart) vegetable broth (ready-made)
250 ml (9 fl oz) mushroom stock (ready-made)
100 g (3.5 oz) herbs and vegetables for making soup (frozen)
80 g (2.75 oz) broccoli (frozen)
80 g (2.75 oz) cauliflower crowns (frozen)
80 g (2.75 oz) French beans (tinned)
salt & pepper
ground allspice and caraway seed
100 g (3.5 oz) soup noodles
1/2 bunch curly parsley
200 g (7 oz) herb crème fraîche

Minute 1
Combine the stocks in a pot and bring to the boil. Add all the herbs and vegetables. Simmer for about 12–15 minutes.

Minute 18
Season the soup with salt, pepper, allspice and caraway.

Minute 19
Add the soup noodles and cook a further 5–7 minutes. Wash, dry and mince the parsley.

Minute 26
Blend the parsley into the crème fraîche. Ladle the soup onto plates. Garnish with a dab of the crème fraîche and serve.

38

RICE STEW

Preparation time: about 30 minutes
Serves 4

200 g (7 oz) wholegrain rice
250 g (9 oz) Brussels sprouts (frozen)
1 celery root
4 small white turnips
3–4 tbsp walnut oil
1 l (1 quart) vegetable broth (ready-made)
salt
pepper
freshly ground nutmeg
1 bunch chervil

Minute 1
Prepare the rice according to package instructions. Thaw the Brussels sprouts.

Minute 4
Peel the celery and turnips and cut into small cubes. Heat the walnut oil in a pot and sauté all the vegetables in it for about 4–5 minutes.

Minute 10
Pour on the vegetable broth and cook everything at low heat for 15–20 minutes.

Minute 25
Drain the rice well and add it to the soup. Season with salt, pepper and nutmeg.

Minute 28
Wash, dry and mince the chervil. Serve the rice stew garnished with chervil.

VEGETARIAN DISHES

Enjoying food without meat is easy in low-fat cuisine. With fresh vegetables or mushrooms, delicious pasta and aromatic rice your culinary imagination will know no bounds.

QUESADILLAS

Preparation time: about 30 minutes
Serves 4

4 tortillas
2 tbsp oil
200 g (7 oz) feta cheese
150 g (5 oz) black olives
150 g (5 oz) maize kernels
1 onion
3 tomatoes
2 cloves garlic
1 green chilli pepper
2 tbsp chilli butter or butter
salt
pepper
chilli powder

Minute 1
Briefly heat the tortillas in a fry pan according to instructions on the package.
Minute 10
Drain the feta cheese and cut it into cubes. Drain and halve the olives. Drain the maize.
Minute 13
Peel and dice the onions. Wash, trim and chop the tomatoes.
Minute 16
Peel the garlic and press through a garlic press. Clean and trim the chilli peppers. Cut in half lengthwise and remove seeds. Cut into strips.
Minute 20
Heat the chilli butter and fry the vegetables in it for about 4 minutes. Add salt, pepper and chilli powder to taste.
Minute 25
Divide the vegetables among the 4 tortillas, roll up and serve.

POTATO CASSEROLE

Preparation time: about 20 minutes
Serves 4

800 g (1 lb 12 oz) potatoes
5 red onions
200 g (7 oz) chanterelle mushrooms (tinned)
2 tbsp clarified butter
4 tbsp cranberry jam
4 tbsp aquavit
salt & pepper
ground aniseed
ground cloves
ground allspice
1 tbsp raspberry vinegar
butter to grease baking dish
125 ml (4 fl oz) cream
250 ml (9 fl oz) milk
1 egg

Minute 1

Peel the potatoes and cut into small strips. Peel and dice the onion. Drain the mushrooms in a sieve.

Minute 11

Heat the clarified butter in a fry pan. Sauté the onions and mushrooms. Add the jam and aquavit. Season with salt, pepper, aniseed, clove and allspice to taste. Stir in vinegar. Remove from stove and allow to draw.

Minute 15

Heat oven to 150 °C/300 °F/gas mark 2. Grease an ovenproof casserole dish with butter and fill with half of the potato sticks. Spread the onion and chanterelle mixture on top. Cover with the rest of the potatoes. Mix the cream, milk and egg together. Add salt and pepper. Pour 3/4 of the milk mixture over the casserole. Bake in the centre of the oven for about 10 minutes. Pour over the rest of the liquid and bake a further 5 minutes at 210 °C/410 °F/gas mark 6–7.

TERIYAKI NOODLES

Preparation time: about 25 minutes
Serves 4

250 g (9 oz) rigatoni
1 bunch spring onions
250 g (9 oz) Chinese mushrooms
250 g (9 oz) snow peas
250 g (9 oz) mung bean sprouts
4 tbsp sesame oil
100 g (3.5 oz) water chestnuts
250 ml (9 fl oz) Asian stock (ready-made)
125 ml (4 fl oz) rice wine
125 ml (4 fl oz) teriyaki sauce (ready-made)
salt
pepper
ground ginger
dried mustard

Minute 1
Cook noodles according to package instructions until they are al dente. Drain and pour cold water on them. Drain well, then keep heated.

Minute 3
Trim, wash and dry the spring onions, mushrooms, snow peas and bean sprouts as needed. Cut the spring onions into thin rings. Chop the mushrooms. Heat the oil in a fry pan and sauté the vegetables for 6–8 minutes.

Minute 18
Drain the water chestnuts in a sieve. Cut them in half and add to the fry pan along with the stock, rice wine, teriyaki sauce and vegetables. Cook all ingredients together at low heat for about 2–3 minutes.

Minute 24
Add spices to taste and gently stir the noodles into the mixture. Arrange on plates and serve.

Vegetarian dishes

PENNE WITH FENNEL CREAM

Preparation time: about 30 minutes
Serves 4

200 g (7 oz) penne
2 bulbs fennel
200g (7 oz) sweet potatoes
(jarred or tinned)
3–4 tbsp olive oil
salt
pepper
ground aniseed
ground cloves
ground allspice
500 ml (17 fl oz) vegetable broth
4–5 tbsp sour cream
butter or oil to grease the dish
100 g (3.5 oz) shredded
Appenzeller cheese

Minute 1
Cook the pasta according to
instructions on the package.
Clean and trim the fennel bulbs
and chop finely, including the
fennel greens.

Minute 5
Put sweet potatoes in a sieve and
drain well. Cut into cubes.

Minute 8
Heat the oil in a pan and braise
the vegetables for about 10
minutes. Then mash the vegetables with a fork and add spices
to taste.

Minute 19
Add the vegetable broth to the
pan and heat everything through

over low heat for 2–3 minutes.
Gently stir the sour cream into
the mix.

Minute 22
Preheat the oven to 220 °C/
425 °F/gas mark 7. Grease a
shallow ovenproof dish. Place
pasta in the dish and top with
the fennel cream.

Minute 24
Sprinkle the cheese over top and
put on the upper rack of the oven
for 5–6 minutes.

46

RED GARLIC PILAF

Preparation time: about 25 minutes
Serves 4

125 ml (4 fl oz) red beetroot juice
125 ml (4 fl oz) red wine
250 ml (9 fl oz) vegetable broth (ready-made)
200 g (7 oz) risotto rice
8 cloves garlic
4–5 tbsp olive oil
250 g (9 oz) red beetroot slices (jarred or tinned)
200 g (7 oz) small corncobs (jarred)
200 g (7 oz) pickled onions (jarred)
salt & pepper
ground cardamom
ground coriander

Minute 1
In a pot combine the red beetroot juice, red wine and vegetable broth. Bring to the boil, add rice and simmer about 20 minutes.

Minute 3
Peel and dice the garlic. Heat the oil in a fry pan and sauté the garlic for 5–6 minutes. Put the jarred vegetables in a sieve and drain well.

Minute 12
Cut the small corncobs in half and add all the vegetables to the fry pan with the garlic. Braise the mixture for about 2–3 minutes.

Minute 22
Carefully stir the vegetables into the cooked rice. Heat everything through and add spices to taste. Serve immediately.

Minute 12

DELICATE RICE GRATIN

Preparation time: about 30 minutes
Serves 4

400 g (14 oz) peeled tomatoes (tinned)
100 g (3.5 oz) onion-garlic mixture (frozen)
1 tsp sage
1 tsp rosemary
2–3 tbsp olive oil
salt
pepper
200 g (7 oz) maize kernels (frozen)
200 g (7 oz) peas (frozen)
125 ml (4 fl oz) vegetable broth (ready-made)
2–3 tbsp red wine
250 g (9 oz) five-minute rice
butter or oil to grease the dish
150–200 g (5–7 oz) shredded pepper Gouda

Minute 1
Combine tomatoes with the onion-garlic mixture and herbs.

Minute 3
Heat the oil in a saucepan and braise the mix in it for 3–4 minutes. Generously salt and pepper.

Minute 7
Add the maize, peas, stock and red wine to the pan. Simmer over low heat for about 4–5 minutes.

Minute 14
Cook rice according to package instructions. Preheat the oven to 225 °C/440 °F/gas mark 7–8.

Minute 21
Greast an ovenproof dish. Turn the rice into it, then the vegetable mix. Sprinkle the cheese over top. Bake the gratin in the centre of the oven for about 6–9 minutes.

MACARONI "DIABOLO"

Preparation time: about 20 minutes
Serves 4

450 g (1 lb) macaroni
4 red chilli peppers
100 g (3.5 oz) onion-garlic mix (frozen)
100 g (3.5 oz) Italian herb mix (frozen)
1 tbsp chilli oil
3 tbsp peanut oil
200 g (7 oz) tomato al gusto with herbs (tinned)
salt
cayenne
500 ml (17 fl oz) vegetable broth (ready-made)
125 ml (4 fl oz) red wine
1–2 tbsp capers
2–3 tbsp sour cream
chilli sauce to taste

Minute 1
Cook macaroni according to instructions on package. Clean and trim the chilli peppers. Cut in half and remove seeds, then cut into small cubes.

Minute 4
Sauté the chilli, onion-garlic mix and herb mix in heated chilli and peanut oils for 4–6 minutes. Pour in the tomatoes, then season with salt and cayenne.

Minute 10
Add the stock, red wine and capers and cook over a low heat for about 8–10 minutes.

Minute 19
Stir in the sour cream and add chilli sauce to taste. Arrange pasta and sauce on the plates and serve.

ASPARAGUS ON PAPPARDELLE

Preparation time: about 25 minutes
Serves 4

300 g (10 oz) pappardelle
(wide flat noodles)

1.5 kg (3 lb 5 oz) asparagus

1 l (1 quart) vegetable broth
(ready-made)

5 shallots

5 tbsp raspberry vinegar

2 tbsp sweet mustard

2 tbsp lemon rind

2 tbsp eight-herb mix

salt

pepper

sugar

1 small package saffron threads

3 tbsp olive oil

Minute 1
Prepare pasta according to package instructions. Wash the asparagus and peel two-thirds down the stems. Heat the stock and cook asparagus in it over low heat for about 8 minutes.

Minute 15
Peel and finely chop the shallots. In a saucepan, combine the raspberry vinegar with 5–6 tbsp asparagus broth, the mustard, lemon rind and herbs. Add spices and sugar to taste. Stir in the shallots.

Minute 19
Blend the saffron into the olive oil and fold into cooked pasta.

Minute 22
Put portions of pasta onto the plates. Cut asparagus in half and arrange on top. Drizzle over the hot marinade and serve immediately.

HEARTY MUSHROOM FRY-UP

Preparation time: about 15 minutes
Serves 4

100 g (3.5 oz) wild mushrooms
1 onion
100 g (3.5 oz) soy sausage
3 tbsp butter
salt
freshly ground pepper
2 tbsp chopped curly parsley
4 slices pumpernickel bread

Minute 1
Clean and trim the mushrooms and chop them. Peel the onions and cut into rings.

Minute 5
Cut the soy sausage into small cubes. Heat the butter in a fry pan.

Minute 9
Add the soy sausage cubes and brown it for a short time. Add the sliced onions and mushrooms. Season with salt and pepper to taste.

Minute 14
Arrange the mushroom skillet on plates. Sprinkle the chopped parsley over top and serve with pumpernickel bread.

QUICK VEGETABLE SHISH KEBABS

Preparation time: about 25 minutes
Serves 4

1 medium courgette
1 red bell pepper
3–4 pink mushroom crowns
2 corncobs (tinned)
2 medium onions
4 tbsp olive oil
1 tsp Worcestershire sauce
1 tsp medium-hot mustard
1 tsp tomato ketchup
1 tbsp herbs de Provence

Minute 1
Rinse and trim the courgette, pepper and mushrooms. Cut the courgette and corncobs in fairly thick slices.

Minute 5
Cut the pepper into bite-sized pieces. Peel the onions and cut into wedges.

Minute 8
Thread alternating vegetables and mushrooms onto metal skewers.

Minute 12
In a small bowl, whisk together the oil, Worcestershire sauce, mustard, ketchup and herbs. Brush this mixture on the vegetable shisk kebabs.

Minute 15
Cook the shish kebabs on the grill for about 10 minutes. Turn skewers occasionally, and brush several times with the herb-oil mixture.

KOHLRABI GRATIN

Preparation time: about 20 minutes (plus baking time)
Serves 4

1 kg (2 lb 3 oz) kohlrabi
800 g (1 lb 12 oz) tomatoes
salt
1 onion
1 clove garlic
3 tbsp oil
freshly ground pepper
1/2 tsp sugar
1 tsp vegetable base
butter to grease the dish
250 g (9 oz) mozzarella cheese
1 tbsp pine nuts
50 g (1.75 oz) pecorino cheese

Minute 1
Trim and peel the kohlrabi. Cut into strips. Wash and score the skin of the tomatoes, dip in boiling water and then remove the skin. Chop the tomatoes. Preheat the oven to 190 °C/ 375 °F/gas mark 5.

Minute 7
Cook the kohlrabi in lightly salted water for about 5 minutes. Peel and cube the onion. Peel the garlic and press through a garlic press.

Minute 13
Heat the oil in a fry pan. Sauté the onion and garlic. Season with salt and pepper, the sugar and vegetable base.

Minute 16
Stir the tomatoes into the fry pan. Grease an ovenproof dish with butter. Put the kohlrabi and toma-to mixture into the dish. Slice the mozzarella and layer it on top.

Minute 19
Sprinkle the pine nuts and pecorino cheese over the top. Bake the dish in the centre of the oven for about 20 minutes.

Minute 1

Minute 7

Minute 13

Minute 16

SPANISH VOL-AU-VENTS

Preparation time: about 30 minutes
Serves 4

300 g (10 oz) peas (frozen)
500 g (17 oz) carrots
1 clove garlic
30 g (1 oz) butter
salt
pepper
1 tsp sugar
2 hard-cooked eggs
1 bunch curly parsley
100 g (3.5 oz) crème fraîche
2 tbsp olive oil
4 vol-au-vent shells

Minute 1
Thaw the peas. Peel and trim the carrots, then slice. Peel and chop the garlic.

Minute 8
Preheat the oven to 120 °C/ 250 °F/gas mark 1–2. Heat the butter in a fry pan and sauté the carrots for a minute or two, then add the peas and garlic. Add salt, pepper and sugar.

Minute 12
Peel and finely chop the eggs. Wash and dry the parsley, then mince.

Minute 16
In a small bowl, combine the crème fraiche, olive oil, eggs and parsley. Season with salt and pepper to taste. Fill the pastry shells with the vegetables and top with some of the crème fraîche mix. Bake in the centre of the oven for about 10 minutes.

POULTRY DISHES

Let us entice you to enjoy low-fat and easy
cuisine with our new gourmet recipes.
How about tender guinea fowl breast,
a fruity poultry curry or
elegant poultry roll-ups?

COQ AU VIN

Preparation time: about 20 minutes
Serves 4

300 g (10 oz) onions
800 g (1 lb 12 oz) chicken breast fillet
3 tbsp oil
300 g (10 oz) mushrooms
salt
pepper
paprika
500 ml (17 oz) white wine
cornflour for thickening
parsley to garnish

Minute 1
Peel the onions and cut into rings. Wash and pat dry the meat and cut into cubes.

Minute 5
Heat the oil in a fry pan. Sauté the onions and chicken for about 6 minutes.

Minute 8
In the meantime, clean and trim the mushrooms. Slice them and add to the pan. Season with salt, pepper and paprika to taste.

Minute 13
Pour on the white wine and let simmer over low heat for about 6 minutes.

Minute 19
Thicken the sauce with cornflour and serve garnished with parsley, accompanied by fresh baguette.

Minute 8

NASI RAMES

Preparation time: about 20 minutes
Serves 4

400 g (14 oz) five-minute rice
800 g (1 lb 12 oz)
chicken breast fillet
salt & pepper
chilli powder
4 tbsp peanut oil
200 ml (7 fl oz) ketchup
6 tbsp peanut butter
cornflour
1 red chilli pepper
200 g (7 oz) spring onions
2 tbsp butter

Minute 1
Cook the rice according to the instructions on the package. Wash and pat dry the chicken. Cut it into cubes, then season with salt, pepper and chilli powder. Heat the oil in a fry pan and brown the chicken for about 6 minutes.

Minute 9
Pour in the ketchup and some water. Stir in the peanut butter and let simmer for a further 6 minutes. If necessary, thicken the sauce with a little cornflour.

Minute 11
In the meantime, wash the chilli pepper. Cut in half and remove the seeds. Cut into small pieces. Clean and trim the spring onions, then chop finely.

Minute 16
Drain the rice. Heat the butter in a second pan and sauté the rice, chilli and spring onions.

Minute 19
Add salt, pepper and chilli powder to taste. Arrange the chicken and rice on plates. A fresh salad compliments this dish nicely.

TURKEY ROULADES

Preparation time: about 30 minutes
Serves 4

250 g (9 oz) feta cheese
150 g (5 oz) pitted black olives
150 g (5 oz) pitted green olives
6 tbsp tomato paste
1 tbsp minced fresh mint
1 tbsp minced fresh basil
8 thinly cut turkey breast fillets
(about 100 g/3.5 oz each)
salt
pepper
3 tbsp olive oil
250 ml (9 fl oz) red wine
250 ml (9 fl oz) chicken stock
4 tbsp yoghurt

Minute 1
Mash the cheese with a fork in a small bowl. Drain and slice all the olives. Stir them into the cheese with the tomato paste and herbs.

Minute 4
Rinse and pat dry the turkey breast. Salt and pepper.

Minute 6
Brush the olive mixture on the fillets, roll up and secure with wooden tooth picks.

Minute 8
Heat the oil in a fry pan and brown the poultry rolls on all sides for about 10 minutes.

Minute 19
Add the red wine and stock to the pan. Simmer for about 5 minutes. Take poultry rolls out of the pan and keep warm.

Minute 25
Stir the yoghurt into the liquid in the pan. Again salt and pepper to taste.

Minute 29
Arrange turkey roulades on plates with sauce. Serve with flat bread.

 **Poultry dishes**

BRATWURST SALAD

Preparation time: about 20 minutes
Serves 4

3 red onions
3 each yellow, green and red
bell peppers
2 cloves garlic
1 tbsp olive oil
4 chicken or turkey bratwurst
(or other sausages)
2 tbsp lemon juice
salt
pepper
ground paprika
2 tbsp each chopped basil, oregano
and parsley

Minute 1
Peel the onions and cut into rings.
Clean and trim the peppers, cut
them lengthwise, remove seeds
and cut into thin strips.

Minute 5
Peel the garlic and put through a
garlic press. Heat the oil in a fry
pan and brown the sausages for
about 5 minutes.

Minute 12
Add the onions, pepper strips,
and garlic to the pan. Stir in the
lemon juice and season with salt,
pepper and paprika.

Minute 14
Mix in the herbs. Braise everything for about 5 minutes.

Minute 20
Arrange the vegetables on plates
and top with pieces of sausage.

GUINEA FOWL À L'ORANGE

Preparation time: about 20 minutes
Serves 4

4 small Guinea fowl breasts with skin
4 cloves garlic
salt
2 tbsp olive oil
2 tbsp lemon rind
3 tbsp lemon juice
2 tbsp crumbled chilli pepper
1 tbsp pickled ginger
2 oranges
125 ml (4 fl oz) orange juice
125 ml (4 fl oz) white rum
pepper
cornflour

Minute 1
Wash and dry the meat. With a sharp knife, make several diagonal cuts into the skin.

Minute 3
Peel the garlic and mash it with salt. Brush the mix onto the meat.

Minute 6
Heat the olive oil and pan fry the breasts from all sides for about 5 minutes.

Minute 8
In the meantime, combine the lemon rind, lemon juice, chilli pepper and ginger.

Minute 10
Peel the oranges, removing the white skin as well. Cut oranges into slices. Mix the orange juice and rum and add some salt and pepper. Combine with the lemon mixture.

Minute 15
Remove the meat from the pan and keep warm. Pour the orange juice into the fry pan, briefly bring to the boil and thicken the sauce with cornflour to the desired consistency. Serve with wholegrain rice.

FRUITY POULTRY CURRY

Preparation time: about 20 minutes
Serves 4

2 bunches spring onions
3 tbsp sesame oil
3 tbsp red curry paste
600 g (1 lb 5 oz) turkey meat
4 tbsp apricot jam
250 ml (9 fl oz) Asian stock
200 g (7 oz) mandarin oranges (tinned)
2 bananas
200 g (7 oz) yoghurt
salt
pepper

Minute 1
Peel the spring onions and cut into rings. Heat the oil in a fry pan and sauté the onions for about 4 minutes. Stir in the curry paste.

Minute 6
Cut the meat into bite-sized pieces and add to the pan. Stir in the jam and stock. Let everything simmer at a low heat for about 10 minutes, stirring occasionally.

Minute 15
Drain the mandarines. Peel the bananas and cut into slices. Add both just before the meat is cooked and heat through.

Minute 20
Stir in the yoghurt and salt and pepper to taste. Serve the curry with rice-flour noodles.

Minute 1

CRAB-STUFFED CHICKEN

Preparation time: about 20 minutes
Serves 4

350 g (12 oz) crab meat (tinned)
200 g (7 oz) tomato purée
5 tbsp crumbled cornflakes
1 tbsp lemon juice
6 tbsp shredded parmesan cheese
3 tbsp finely chopped onions
salt, pepper
paprika
3 tbsp chopped fresh parsley
4 chicken breast fillets without skin
4 tbsp flour
3 tbsp peanut oil

Minute 1
Drain the crab meat in a sieve, then combine crab meat with the tomato purée, cornflakes, lemon juice, cheese and onions to make the filling. Season with salt, pepper and paprika.

Minute 4
Carefully blend the parsley into the mix. Wash and pat dry the chicken breasts. Use a sharp knife to cut a pocket into each breast.

Minute 7
Place small portions of the filling in each chicken breast and secure with a wooden skewer.

Minute 10
Dredge the chicken breasts in the flour. Heat the oil in a fry pan and cook the chicken breasts on all sides for about 5 minutes. Fresh potato salad compliments this meal very nicely.

DUCK BREAST WITH FENNEL

Preparation time: about 30 minutes
Serves 4

4 small duck breast fillets with skin
salt
pepper
1/2 tsp each ground cardamom, coriander and cloves
3 tbsp sesame oil
3 small fennel bulbs
3 pears
2 tbsp lemon juice
4 shallots
butter to grease the dish
250 ml (9 fl oz) white wine
freshly ground nutmeg
250 ml (9 fl oz) pear juice

Minute 1
Preheat the oven to 180 °C/ 355 °F/gas mark 4. Score the skin of each breast and rub in the spices. Heat the oil and brown for about 5 minutes on each side. In the meantime wash, trim and slice the fennel. Finely chop the fennel greens. Peel and halve the pears. Remove seeds and cut into cubes. Drizzle the lemon juice over the fennel and pears. Peel and finely chop the shallots and add to the mix.

Minute 10
Place the duck breasts in a greased baking dish with the skin side up. Bake in the centre of the oven for about 5 minutes. Pour over the white wine and let simmer a further 10 minutes. Reheat the juices left in the fry pan and sauté the fruit-vegetable mixture in it. Add salt, pepper, nutmeg and the pear juice. Let simmer for about 6 minutes. Remove the meat from the oven and let stand for a bit before slicing. Arrange on plates and serve with the sauce and vegetable compote.

Minute 1

Minute 3

Minute 6

Minute 9

QUICK POULTRY-HERB RISOTTO

Preparation time: about 20 minutes
Serves 4

250 g (9 oz) five-minute rice
500 g (17 oz) turkey breast
2 tbsp olive oil
6 tbsp tomato purée
280 g (10 oz) cream of chicken soup (tinned)
2 tbsp each freshly chopped basil, oregano and thyme
salt
pepper
80 ml (2.5 fl oz) chicken stock

Minute 1
Cook the rice according to instructions on package.

Minute 3
Wash the turkey breasts and cut into cubes.

Minute 5
Heat the oil and stir fry the meat in it, stirring frequently, for about 5 minutes.

Minute 10
Add the tomato purée and soup to the fry pan. Stir in the herbs and let everything cook at a low heat for about 8 minutes.

Minute 18
Fold the cooked rice into the mix and add salt and pepper. Add some chicken stock, if desired. Serve immediately.

 **Poultry dishes**

THAI DRUMSTICKS

Preparation time: about 25 minutes
Serves 4

8 drumsticks
1 l (1 quart) Asia stock
100 ml (3 fl oz) soy sauce
6 tbsp dry sherry
6 tbsp oyster sauce
3 tbsp sesame oil
3 tbsp maple syrup
4 tbsp chilli sauce
2 tbsp lemon juice
2 shallots
4 cloves garlic
2 tbsp freshly ground coriander
to garnish

Minute 1
Wash and dry the drumsticks.
Remove the skin. In a pot, heat
the stock together with half of the
soy sauce. Add the drumsticks
to the pot and allow to draw for
about 10 minutes.

Minute 4
In the meantime, combine the
rest of the soy sauce with the
sherry, oyster sauce, sesame
oil, maple syrup, chilli sauce
and lemon juice to make the
marinade.

Minute 6
Peel and finely chop the shallots.
Peel the garlic and press through
a garlic press. Add both to the
marinade.

Minute 14
Drain the drumsticks and then
brush with the marinade. Heat
a fry pan without any fat and
brown the drumsticks on all sides
for about 8 minutes.

Minute 23
Brushing marinade onto the
drumsticks while they cook.
Arrange on plates and serve with
grilled corncobs.

FRIED QUAIL

Preparation time: about 30 minutes
Serves 4

8 quail
3 tbsp clarified butter
salt
pepper
400 g (14 oz) blue grapes
250 ml (9 fl oz) chicken stock
125 ml (4 fl oz) red wine
1 tsp ground cumin
1 tsp ground aniseed
1 tsp ground cloves
3 tbsp ground almonds
8 slices wholegrain bread

Minute 1
Rinse and pat dry the quail. Heat the clarified butter in a cast iron pan and fry quails on all sides for about 8 minutes. Season with salt and pepper.

Minute 6
In the meantime, wash the grapes. Cut them in half and remove any seeds.

Minute 11
Add the grapes, stock and wine to the quail and let simmer for about 10 minutes. Add the cumin, aniseed and cloves.

Minute 22
Remove the quail from the pan and keep warm. Stir the almonds into the sauce in the pan.

Minute 25
Toast the bread slices and spread the grape mix on them. Arrange on the plates with quail and serve. This dish goes well with rice.

TURKEY STEAK & EGGS

Preparation time: about 20 minutes
Serves 4

4 slices turkey breast (about 2 cm/
3/4 inch thick, luncheon meat)
butter to grease the pan
2 tbsp olive oil
2 tbsp grainy mustard
2 tbsp maple syrup
4 tbsp quince jelly
4 portions instant mashed potatoes
1/2 tsp ground rosemary
1 tbsp sunflower seed oil
4 eggs
salt

Minute 1
Place turkey slices in a greased dish. In a bowl, whisk together the oil, mustard, syrup and jelly.

Minute 4
Spread this mixture over the turkey slices and grill the whole dish for about 8 minutes.

Minute 7
In the meantime, prepare the mashed potatoes according to package instructions. Stir in the rosemary.

Minute 15
Heat the oil in a fry pan and fry four eggs, sunny side up. Add salt.

Minute 19
On each plate arrange a serving of mashed potatoes, meat and eggs and serve.

CHICKEN LIVERS IN CAPER SAUCE

Preparation time: about 25 minutes
Serves 4

1 bunch spring onions
3 cloves garlic
2 tbsp olive oil
800 g (1 lb 12 oz) chicken liver
salt & pepper
125 ml (4 fl oz) white wine
250 ml (9 fl oz) chicken stock
250 ml (9 fl oz) mushroom stock
3 tbsp capers
2 tbsp sweet mustard
3 tbsp chopped parsley
200 g (7 oz) yoghurt

Minute 1
Clean and trim the spring onions, then cut them into rings. Peel and finely chop the garlic.

Minute 5
Heat the oil in a fry pan and sauté the spring onions and garlic. Rinse and pat dry the liver and add it to the pan. Generously salt and pepper. Brown for about 9 minutes.

Minute 16
Remove the meat from the pan and keep it warm. Add the wine and both kinds of stock to the pan and bring to the boil, then continue to cook at low heat. Add the capers, mustard and parsley.

Minute 20
Season with salt and pepper. Stir in the yoghurt after about 4 minutes. Put the liver back in the sauce to heat it and serve immediately. Boiled potatoes compliment this dish.

Minute 5

BAKED POULARD BREASTS

Preparation time: about 30 minutes
Serves 4

4 small poulard breasts (about 250 g/ 8.5 oz each)
salt
pepper
flour
3 tbsp clarified butter
butter to grease dish
250 g (9 oz) mozzarella
1 truffle (tinned)
8 slices Parma ham
5 tbsp pecorino cheese
100 ml (3 fl oz) chicken stock
250 g (9 oz) fettucini, cooked
100 g (3.5 oz) tomato purée
1 tbsp fresh chopped sage

Minute 1
Rinse and pat dry the poulard breasts. Make one diagonal cut in each. Wrap the meat in backing parchment and pound until flattened. Salt and pepper both sides of each breast and dredge in flour.

Minute 3
Brush off excess flour. Preheat the oven to 180 °C/355 °F/ gas mark 4. Heat the clarified butter and brown the poulard breasts for about 5 minutes on each side.

Minute 5
In the meantime, grease an ovenproof dish with butter. Drain

the mozzarella and slice it. Shave the truffle into very thin slices. Wrap each piece of meat with two slices of Parma ham. Place the meat roll in the baking dish and top with mozzarella and truffles.

Minute 14
Sprinkle pecorino cheese over everything and pour the stock into the dish. Bake in the centre of the oven for about 10 minutes. Combine the fettucini and tomato purée in a pot and heat. Stir in the sage and season with salt and pepper. Arrange the food on plates and serve.

FISH AND SEAFOOD

Fresh specialties from rivers, lakes and oceans
are wonderfully versatile. They always taste
superb and are easy to digest. The innovative
seafood variations presented here
are easily created, as well.

 **Fish and seafood**

MIE GORENG WITH PRAWNS

Preparation time: about 20 minutes
Serves 4

400 g (14 oz) Chinese vegetable
mix (frozen)

450 g (1 lb) Bami noodles
(ready-made)

2 tbsp butter

250 g (9 oz) prawns

2 cloves garlic

salt

pepper

paprika

Minute 1
Thaw vegetables according to
instructions on package.

Minute 4
Cook the noodles according to
package instructions. Heat the
butter in a fry pan and sauté
the vegetables. Add the prawns.

Minute 10
Peel the garlic, press through
a garlic press and stir into the
sautéing vegetables. Season
with salt, pepper and paprika
to taste.

Minute 14
Drain the noodles, rinse in cold
water and drain again. Add
the noodles to the vegetables
and adjust the seasoning as
necessary.

Minute 19
Arrange the food on plates and
serve.

Minute 4

FISH WITH TOMATO

Preparation time: about 30 minutes
Serves 4

750 g (1 lb 10 oz) beefsteak tomatoes
500 g (17 oz) plaice fillets
lemon juice
2 tbsp olive oil
salt & freshly ground pepper
1 sprig sage
1 clove garlic
1 piece fresh ginger
1/2 tsp cayenne
1/2 tsp sweet paprika
1 tbsp brown sugar
1 tbsp red wine vinegar

Minute 1
Rinse the tomatoes. Score their skins, dip briefly in boiling water and remove the skin. Cut in slices.

Minute 4
Wash and dab dry the plaice fillets then drizzle lemon juice over them.

Minute 7
Heat the oil in a fry pan. Fry the fish on both sides for about 6 minutes (total). Salt and pepper.

Minute 9
In the meantime, wash and dry the sage. Pluck off small leaves.

Peel and finely chop the garlic. Grate the ginger. Sprinkle garlic and ginger on top of the tomato slices. Add salt, pepper and the cayenne and paprika.

Minute 14
Place the tomato slices on top of the fish fillets in the pan. Distribute the sage leaves over top. Whisk the brown sugar and vinegar and drizzle over the fish. Braise everything in the fry pan with a tighly fitting lid for about 15 minutes.

TEMARI SUSHI

Preparation time: about 30 minutes
Serves 4

200 g (7 oz) herring
4 tbsp mirin
200 g (7 oz) cooked and separated crayfish tail
2 nori sheets
100 g (3.5 oz) cooked and chopped shrimp
vinegar-water for sprinkling onto work area
wasabi paste
400 g (14 oz) prepared sushi rice

Minute 1
Rinse the herring in water, then dry and cut into very thin slices. Drizzle mirin over the crayfish tails and allow to draw for about 5 minutes, then cut into very thin slices.

Minute 9
Toast the nori sheets in a fry pan without oil. Cut into pieces about 4 cm (1 1/2 in) in size. Distribute the shrimp on the nori leaves.

Minute 13
Cover your work area with a sufficiently large piece of cling film (20 x 20 cm/8x8 in) and sprinkle it with vinegar-water. Layer slices of filling—nori, herring and crayfish—on top. Spread a dab of wasabi paste on it and top with a small ball of rice.

Minute 25
While twisting the corners of the cling film together, carefully roll the mixture on the work surface until you get a small ball. Remove the cling film.

Minute 28
Cut an "x" into the top of the nori balls and push them apart a bit before serving. Serve garnished with herbs, caviar, carrots and radish salad.

PLAICE SHISH KEBABS

Preparation time: about 30 minutes
Serves 4

8 plaice fillets
6 tbsp olive oil
4 tbsp lemon juice
freshly ground pepper
1 bunch thyme
1 sprig rosemary
1 red bell pepper
1 yellow bell pepper
12 cherry tomatoes
50 g (1.75 oz) cream cheese
salt
oil for grilling

Minute 1
Rinse and pat dry the fish fillets. Preheat the oven to 180 °C/ 355 °F/gas mark 4. In a bowl, mix the oil with 3 tbsp lemon juice. Add pepper. Rinse and pat dry the herbs and pull off leaves or needles. Stir 1 tbsp thyme and the 1 tbsp rosemary into the marinade. Put the rest aside. Marinate the fish and allow to draw for about 5 minutes.

Minute 10
Wash and trim the peppers. Roast them in the centre of the oven until the skin is slightly brown and separates. Peel them and cut into pieces. Rinse and trim the tomatoes. Cut in half. Mix cream cheese with the rest of the lemon juice and herbs. Add salt and pepper.

Minute 20
Oil a grilling rack. Roll and secure the fish fillets. Alternate fish rolls, pepper pieces and tomato halves on metal skewers. Sprinkle with salt and pepper. Grill the shish kebabs on all sides for about 5 minutes. Dress skewers with herb sauce on plates and serve.

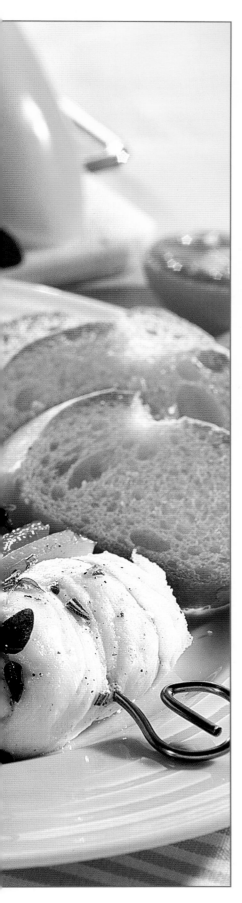

TURBOT ROLLS

Preparation time: about 20 minutes
Serves 4

4 turbot fillets
150 g (5 oz) mushrooms
12 lichees
salt
freshly ground pepper
sweet paprika
lemon juice
2 tbsp olive oil
1 tbsp butter
2 tbsp double cream
2 tbsp cognac
2 tbsp maple syrup

Minute 1
Wash turbot fillets and dab dry.
Clean and trim the mushrooms.
Cut into slices. Peel and chop the
lichees.
Minute 6
Put mushroom slices and lichees
on top of each fish fillet. Season

with salt, pepper and paprika.
Drizzle lemon juice on top.
Minute 9
Roll up the fish fillets and secure
with wooden skewers. Heat the
oil in a fry pan and fry the fish
rolls until crispy.
Minute 14
Remove the fish rolls from the fry
pan and keep warm. Add the
butter to the fry pan and melt,
then stir in the double cream,
cognac and maple syrup. Salt
and pepper.
Minute 18
Arrange the fish rolls on plates,
top with some of the sauce and
serve. Spaghetti compliments
this dish well.

FISH NUGGETS

Preparation time: about 25 minutes
Serves 4

1 kg (2 lb 3 oz) catfish
2 tbsp lemon juice
salt & pepper
2 eggs
150 g (5 oz) bread crumbs
fat for deep frying
200 g (7 oz) yoghurt
3 tbsp sweet mustard
2 tbsp beer
ground caraway, paprika
200 g (7 oz) sour milk
1 tbsp cream
1 red bell pepper
100 g (3.5 oz) sour cream
8 tbsp buttermilk
1–2 tbsp curry powder
2–3 tbsp mixed pickles

Minute 1
Cut the fish into mid-sized pieces. Drizzle with lemon juice and sprinkle with salt and pepper.

Minute 3
Beat the eggs and coat fish pieces first in the egg wash, then in bread crumbs. Deep fry portions in hot fat until golden brown. Lie on kitchen paper to catch excess fat and keep warm.

Minute 15
Blend the yoghurt, mustard and beer until smooth. Add salt, pepper, caraway and paprika to taste.

Minute 18
Mix the sour milk and cream. Rinse, trim and halve the bell pepper. Finely dice the pepper, stir into the dip. Salt and pepper.

Minute 21
Combine the sour cream and buttermilk until smooth. Add salt, pepper and curry powder to taste. Drain the mixed pickles well, cut into cubes and blend in. Arrange fish nuggets with dips on plates and serve.

SALMON SHISH KEBABS

Preparation time: about 20 minutes
Serves 4

600 g (1 lb 5 oz) salmon fillet
1 tbsp lemon juice
6 shallots
1 red bell pepper
1/2 courgette
200 g (7 oz) fresh, peeled jumbo prawns
salt
pepper
ground cardamom and ginger
5–6 tbsp sesame oil

Minute 1
Rinse and pat dry the salomon. Cut into medium-sized cubes. Drizzle the lemon juice over top.

Minute 4
Peel and halve the shallots. Wash and trim the pepper and cut it in pieces. Clean and trim the courgette, then slice it.

Minute 8
Alternately thread chunks of fish, shallots, pepper and jumbo prawns on metal skewers. Season with salt, pepper, cardamom and ginger.

Minute 12
Heat the oil in a roasting pan and cook the shish kebabs on all sides for about 6–8 minutes. Take out of the pan and serve. Fettucini in dill sauce compliments this dish nicely.

Minute 12

FILLED BANANA LEAVES

Preparation time: about 20 minutes
(plus marinating time)
Serves 4

3 cloves garlic

6 shallots

1 fresh piece ginger (about 2 cm/
3/4 inch)

3 tbsp each soy sauce, hoisin
(Peking sauce) and chilli sauce

1 tsp cane sugar

salt

ground allspice

ground cloves

ground cardamom

250 ml (9 fl oz) coconut milk

700 g (1 lb 8 oz) trout fillet

banana leaves

6–7 tbsp peanut oil

200 (7 oz) plain yoghurt

rice cakes as accompaniment

Minute 1
Peel and finely chop the garlic
and shallots. Peel the ginger
and grate it finely. Combine
everything with the three sauces,
the sugar and spices to taste.
Stir in the coconut milk.

Minute 6
Cut the trout fillet into pieces.
Place in the marinade and allow
to draw for ca. 30 minutes. Put
a few fish pieces on each of the
banana leaves. Fold in the sides
of the leaves and roll up.

Minute 10
Secure the rolls with wooden
skewers. Heat oil and fry the
banana leaves on all sides for
8–10 minutes. Open leaves just
before serving. Arrange with
yoghurt and rice cakes on plates.
Do not eat the banana leaves.

 **Fish and seafood**

PERCH DUMPLINGS

Preparation time: about 25 minutes
Serves 4

400 g (14 oz) Victoria perch fillet
6 slices wholegrain bread, toasted
6 tbsp coconut milk
2 eggs
2 tbsp flour
salt & pepper
ground cardamom, aniseed
and cumin
1/2 bunch parsley
900 ml (1 pt 12 fl oz) fish stock
100 g (3.5 oz) unsalted peanuts
2 cloves garlic
1 tbsp chilli paste
2 tbsp bread crumbs
1 small envelope saffron
125 ml (4 fl oz) dry sherry
6 tbsp walnut oil

Minute 1
Cut the fish into small pieces.
Crumble the toast, mix with the
coconut milk and fish pieces, and
purée in a blender.

Minute 5
Beat the eggs and combine with
flour. Generously spice to taste.
Rinse and pat dry the parsley.
Mince it and add to the bread
and fish mix along with the egg
mix. Blend everything thoroughly.

Minute 9
Form small dumplings. Heat
2/3 of the stock and let the
dumplings simmer in it for about
10 minutes.

Minute 14
Meanwhile, purée the peanuts.
Peel the garlic and add to the
peanuts with the chilli paste,
bread crumbs, saffron, sherry
and oil. Purée everything
thoroughly in a blender. Heat the
remaining fish stock and stir the
nut paste into it. Let the mixture
simmer for 3–4 minutes. Remove
the perch dumplings, drain well
and arrange on plates.

BRAISED PERCH-PIKE

Preparation time: about 30 minutes
Serves 4

4 perch-pike cutlets
1 tbsp lemon juice
salt
pepper
2 tbsp flour
4 tbsp peanut oil
350 ml (12 fl oz) fish stock
40 ml (1.5 fl oz) bourbon whiskey
200 g (7 oz) sour cream
3 tbsp cream horseradish
1/2 bunch dill
lemon wedges for garnish

Minute 1
Rinse and pat dry the fish. Drizzle with the lemon juice. Season with salt and pepper and dredge in flour on both sides.

Minute 4
Heat the oil in a fry pan. Tap excess flour off the fish cutlets and fry the perch-pike in oil for about 3 minutes on each side.

Minute 11
Add half of the fish stock and all the whiskey to the pan. Braise for about 7–9 minutes over low heat.

Minute 20
Remove the fish from the pan and keep warm. Pour the rest of the fish stock into the pan and heat for 3–4 minutes.

Minute 25
Stir the sour cream and horseradish into the stock. Rinse and pat dry the dill, pull off the fine sprigs and mince. Add minced dill to the sauce. Season with salt and pepper to taste.

Minute 29
Place the perch-pike fillets on plates, pour over the sauce and serve with lemon wedges. Potatoes compliment this dish well.

SPICY CRAYFISH

Preparation time: about 15 minutes
Serves 4

500 g (17 oz) boiled and shelled
crayfish

4 cloves garlic

4 dried chilli peppers

125 ml (4 fl oz) spicy sesame oil

1 tbsp chilli oil

Minute 1
Wash and pat dry the crayfish.
Peel and finely chop the garlic.
Crumble the chilli peppers.

Minute 6
Heat the sesame oil and chilli
oil in a fry pan and sauté the
garlic and chilli peppers for
3–4 minutes.

Minute 11
Add the crayfish and stir fry for
about a minute.

Minute 15
This dish goes well with rye
bread, wholegrain bread and
baguette, as well as a fresh
cucumber and tomato salad
with yoghurt.

BAKED LOBSTER

Preparation time: about 20 minutes
Serves 4

2 tbsp liquid honey
3 tbsp coarse mustard
1 tbsp lemon curd
2 tbsp bread crumbs
3 tbsp crème fraîche
1 cooked lobster
butter to grease the dish
1 bunch dill
100 g (3.5 oz) yoghurt
salt & freshly ground pepper
lemon juice

Minute 1
Preheat the oven to 180 °C/
355 °F/gas mark 4. To make a
honey-mustard-coating, combine
the honey, mustard, lemon curd,
bread crumbs, and 1 tbsp crème
fraîche.

Minute 4
Stretch out the lobster on a cutting
board. Separate claws and arms
from the body. Open the claws
with a lobster cracker. Remove
the meat from the claws.

Minute 8
Cut the lobster tail with a knife
and lift meat out of shell. Grease
an ovenproof dish with butter.

Minute 12
Place the lobster meat in the dish
and brush on the honey-mustard
mixture. Bake in the centre of the
oven for about 5 minutes.

Minute 14
Rinse and pat dry the dill. Pull
off individual needles. Stir together the yoghurt and crème
fraîche, then blend in the dill.
Season with salt, pepper and
lemon juice to taste. This dish
goes well with spaghetti.

Minute 1

Minute 4

Minute 8

Minute 12

SALMON GRATIN

Preparation time: about 30 minutes
Serves 4

400 g (14 oz) fennel
salt
200 g (7 oz) salmon fillet
butter to grease the dish
pepper
200 g (7 oz) smoked salmon
1 tbsp oil
2 tbsp lemon juice
80 ml (2.5 fl oz) fish stock
50 g (1.75 oz) grated cheese
2 tbsp caviar

Minute 1
Rinse and trim the fennel, then
cut into small strips. Set aside
the fennel greens. Cook the strips
in lightly salted water for about
5 minutes.

Minute 9
Cut the salmon into cubes.
Preheat the oven to 200 °C/
390 °F/gas mark 6. Grease an
ovenproof dish with butter. Drain
the fennel and put it in the dish.
Sprinkle with salt and pepper.

Minute 12
Distribute salmon cubes and
smoked salmon on top of the
fennel. Drizzle the oil and lemon
juice over the fish. Pour on the
stock and sprinkle cheese on top.

Minute 15
Bake in the centre of the oven
for about 15 minutes. Sprinkle
caviar on top of the gratin
before serving.

MEAT AND GAME DISHES

Hearty and delicious: out-of-the-ordinary recipe suggestions spice up your repertoire of meat dishes. And all of that without much fat. Let us tempt you with lamb chops, medallions of hare or bistro roulades.

Meat and game dishes

STEW WITH HAM

Preparation time: about 25 minutes
Serves 4

800 g (1 lb 12 oz) potatoes
800 g (1 lb 12 oz) carrots
salt
4 tbsp butter
300 ml (10 fl oz) milk
pepper
nutmeg
150 g (5 oz) smoked ham

Minute 1
Peel the potatoes and cut them
into cubes. Peel and dice the
carrots.
Minute 10
Boil the potato and carrot pieces
in lightly salted water for about
10 minutes. Drain the vegetables.
Minute 20
Put potatoes and carrots in one
bowl and mash them slightly. Stir
in the butter and milk.
Minute 23
Add salt, pepper and nutmeg
to taste.
Minute 24
Arrange the food on plates and
serve garnished with the ham.

SAVOY CABBAGE CHOPS

*Preparation time: about 20 minutes
(plus baking time)
Serves 4*

4 pork chops
500 g (17 oz) Savoy cabbage
1 red bell pepper
1 yellow bell pepper
100 g (3.5 oz) celery stalks
1 onion
salt
freshly ground pepper
50 g (2 oz) butter
1 clove garlic
2 eggs
4 tbsp sour cream
2 tbsp bread crumbs

Minute 1
Use a sharp knife to cut a pocket in each pork chop. Clean and trim the cabbage, peppers and celery. Chop into small pieces. Peel and finely dice the onion. Combine all the chopped vegetables in a bowl.

Minute 8
Salt and pepper the pork chops and fill with some of the diced vegetable mix. Secure with wooden skewers.

Minute 11
Preheat the oven to 200 °C/ 390 °F/gas mark 6. Melt most of the butter in a fry pan. Brown the pork chops on both sides for about 8 minutes.

Minute 13
In the meantime, peel the garlic and press through a garlic press. Beat the eggs slightly, then combine with the sour cream and bread crumbs. Stir in the garlic.

Minute 16
Grease an ovenproof dish with butter. Put the remaining vegetables in the dish and pour over the sour cream mixture. Add salt and pepper.

Minute 20
Bake the dish in the oven for about 10 minutes. Arrange a pork chop and some of the vegetables on each plate and serve.

TEX-MEX CHILLI

Preparation time: about 20 minutes
Serves 4

6 red onions
500 g (17 oz) minced beef
2 tbsp olive oil
200 g (7 oz) kidney beans (tinned)
200 g (7 oz) maize kernels (tinned)
300 ml (10 fl oz) tomato juice
4 tbsp chilli sauce
salt
cayenne
ground cumin
1/2 bunch coriander

Minute 1
Peel and finely chop the onions. Combine onions with the mince.

Minute 5
Heat the oil in a large fry pan and brown the mince in it for about 5 minutes.

Minute 8
In the meantime, drain the beans and maize in a sieve. Add the tomato juice and chilli sauce to the meat. Season with salt, cayenne and cumin. Continue to cook a further 8 minutes.

Minute 16
Rinse and dry the coriander, then pull the leaves off the stem. Stir the coriander leaves into the chilli just before it is finished. Serve the chilli with warm tortilla chips.

Minute 8

HARE MEDALLIONS

Preparation time: about 25 minutes
Serves 4

750 g (1 lb 10 oz) hare fillet
2 tbsp clarified butter
salt & pepper
250 ml (9 fl oz) sea buckthorn juice
2 tbsp coarse mustard
250 ml (9 fl oz) game stock
500 g (17 oz) cherries (jarred)
4 tbsp kirsch
1 tsp ground allspice
1 tsp ground cloves
1 tsp ground aniseed

Minute 1
Rinse and pat dry the hare fillet and cut it into medallions. Heat the butter in a fry pan and brown the meat on both sides for about 6 minutes. Add salt and pepper.

Minute 12
Take medallions out of the pan and keep warm. Stir the sea buckthorn juice and mustard into the juices in the pan. Pour in the stock and cook over low heat for about 4 minutes.

Minute 16
Drain the cherries and add, along with the kirsch, to the stock in the fry pan. Stir in the allspice, cloves and aniseed.

Minute 18
Let the mixture simmer for another 3 minutes. Add the medallions to the sauce and braise for about 4 minutes.

Minute 25
Serve the meat on a bed of fusilli and accompanied by the sauce.

Minute 1

Minute 10

Minute 13

Minute 15

RUMP STEAK WITH RAITA

Preparation time: about 20 minutes
Serves 4

4 rump steaks (approx. 200 g/ 7 oz each)
2 tbsp olive oil
salt
pepper
lemon pepper
ground cumin
ground coriander
1 large cucumber
4 red onions
1/2 bunch mint
1 tbsp sugar
400 g (14 oz) yoghurt
6 tbsp buttermilk
lettuce leaves
flat bread

Minute 1
Rinse and pat dry the steaks. Make a few cuts into the fatty side. Heat the oil in a pan and brown the steaks on both sides for 3–5 minutes. Add the salt, pepper, lemon pepper, cumin and coriander.

Minute 10
Wash and peel the cucumber. Cut it in half lengthwise, remove pits and cut into cubes.

Minute 13
Peel and dice the onions. Wash, dry and mince the mint. Combine the cucumber, onion, mint, sugar, yoghurt and buttermilk to make raita. Season with salt and pepper.

Minute 17
Remove the meat from the pan, let it stand a moment and then slice. Garnish plates with lettuce leaves and spread some raita on them.

Minute 20
Arrange the meat on the raita and serve with flat bread.

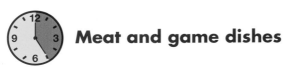

PITA SANDWICHES

Preparation time: about 25 minutes
Serves 4

4 pita breads
200 g (7 oz) pepperoni
200 g (7 oz) ham
250 g (9 oz) tomato purée
200 g (7 oz) marinated antipasto
200 g (7 oz) mild jalapeño peppers (from a jar)
400 g (14 oz) grated gruyere cheese
3 tbsp ground oregano
2 tbsp olive oil

Minute 1
Cut pita breads in half and toast in the oven with the inner side facing up.
Minute 2
In the meantime, cut the pepperoni and ham into cubes.
Minute 5
Brush the inside of each pita bread with tomato purée and top half with ham and half with pepperoni.
Minute 7
Drain the antipasto and jalapeños. Add a layer of both on top of each pita bread.
Minute 9
Sprinkle everything with cheese and oregano. Drizzle some olive oil over the sandwiches.
Minute 11
Put them in the centre of the oven and bake about 12 minutes. Once the cheese has melted, they are ready to serve.

CARIBBEAN STICKS

Preparation time: about 25 minutes
Serves 4

600 g (1 lb 5 oz) pork
flour
2 tbsp peanut oil
salt
pepper
250 g (9 oz) boiled sweet potatoes
2 apples
100 g (3.5 oz) cubed pineapple (tinned)
1 tsp each ground allspice, cumin, coriander and garlic powder
125 ml (4 fl oz) veal stock
2 tbsp lemon juice
1/2 tbsp orange flavouring

Minute 1
Rinse and pat dry the pork. Cut it into thin strips and dust with flour.
Minute 4
Heat the oil in a fry pan and brown the pork in it for about 5 minutes. Season with salt and pepper.
Minute 6
In the meantime, peel and cube the sweet potatoes. Peel, halve and core the apples, then cut the fruit into small cubes.
Minute 12
Drain the pineapple in a sieve. Add the sweet potatoes, apples and pineapple to the meat in the fry pan and continue to cook another 5 minutes or so. Stir in the garlic, pimento, cumin and coriander.
Minute 18
Pour in the veal stock and lemon juice. Stir in the orange flavouring and let simmer for a further 5 minutes. Arrange everything on plates and serve with rice.

BISTRO ROULADES

Preparation time: about 30 minutes
Serves 4

250 g (9 oz) mushrooms
1 bunch spring onions
250 g (9 oz) boiled ham
2 tbsp walnut oil
salt
pepper
8 thin veal cutlets (about 100 g/ 3.5 oz each)
250 g (9 oz) goose foie gras
1 tbsp clarified butter
fresh sage leaves for garnish

Minute 1
Clean, wash and slice the mushrooms. Clean the spring onions and slice into rings. Cut the ham into cubes.

Minute 6
Heat the oil and sauté the mushrooms with the spring onions and ham. Season with salt and pepper.

Minute 8
Rinse and pat dry the veal cutlets. Spread the foie gras on the pieces of veal. Place a portion of the scallion mixture on top of each one.

Minute 10
Carefully roll up the cutlets and secure with wooden skewers. Salt and pepper the outside of each roulade.

Minute 13
Heat the clarified butter and brown the rolls in it on all sides for about 5 minutes. Arrange on plates with baguette. Serve garnished with sage.

Meat and game dishes

LAMB CHOPS WITH MANGO SALSA

Preparation time: about 20 minutes
Serves 4

2 tbsp olive oil
1 tsp ground sage
1 tsp ground rosemary
salt
pepper
1/2 tbsp garlic powder
8 thin lamb chops (approx. 100 g/ 3.5 oz each)
3 mangos
4 red onions
2 green chilli peppers
3 tbsp lemon juice
1/2 bunch mint

Minute 1
Combine the oil, sage and rosemary then season with salt, pepper and the garlic powder to create a marinade.

Minute 3
Rinse and pat dry the lamb chops. Brush marinade on the chops. Heat a fry pan without any fat and brown the lamb chops in it for about 4 minutes. Continue to brush on marinade.

Minute 10
In the meantime, peel the mangos. Remove the pit and cut the fruit into small cubes.

Minute 13
Peel and finely chop the onions. Wash the chilli peppers and halve them lengthwise. Remove the seeds and chop finely.

Minute 17
Combine the fruit and vegetables with the lemon juice and mash a bit with a fork.

Minute 19
Rinse and pat dry the mint. Chop it finely and blend into the mango mix. Season this salsa with salt and pepper. Arrange lamb chops and salsa on plates and serve.

PIQUANT MEATBALLS

Preparation time: about 25 minutes
Serves 4

---

900 g (2 lb) minced meat

salt

pepper

1 tsp chilli powder

1 tsp ground cumin

1 tbsp fresh chopped parsley

1 tbsp fresh chopped thyme

2 tbsp tomato paste

3 onions

3 cloves garlic

2 tbsp peanut oil

Minute 1
Add salt, pepper, chilli powder and cumin to the mince. Knead the chopped herbs and tomato paste into the meat.

Minute 4
Peel and dice the onions. Peel the garlic cloves and pass through a garlic press.

Minute 9
Add the onion and garlic to the minced meat. Form the mixture into 8 meatballs.

Minute 11
Heat oil the and brown the meatballs on all sides for about 15 minutes. Serve them with potato salad.

POACHED VEAL

Preparation time: about 25 minutes
Serves 4

300 ml (10 fl oz) veal stock
125 ml (4 fl oz) lemon juice
100 g (3.5 oz) soup vegetables (frozen)
100 g (3.5 oz) Italian herbs (frozen)
250 ml (9 fl oz) white wine
4 tsp amaretto
1 kg (2 lb 3 oz) veal
2 bunches basil
1 bunch parsley
4 cloves garlic
4 tbsp chopped pine nuts
400 g (14 oz) yoghurt
2 tbsp tomato paste
5 tbsp grated Parmesan cheese
salt
pepper

Minute 1
In a pot, heat the stock together with the lemon juice, soup vegetables, herbs, white wine and amaretto. Bring to the boil.
Minute 4
Rinse and pat dry the meat. Poach it in the veal stock for about 20 minutes.
Minute 6
In the meantime rinse, pat dry, and then mince the basil and parsley. Peel the garlic and put it through a garlic press.
Minute 9
Combine the pine nuts, yoghurt and tomato paste. Stir in the Parmesan and season the dip with salt and pepper.
Minute 24
Remove the meat from the pot and let it rest briefly before slicing. Place veal slices and some of the dip on each plate. Serve with tortellini.

Minute 4

Minute 8

Minute 10

Minute 18

ASIAN MEATBALLS

Preparation time: about 25 minutes
Serves 4

6 shallots
4 cloves garlic
800 g (1 lb 12 oz) minced veal
2 egg yolks
3 tbsp soy sauce
2 tbsp five spice powder
salt
paprika
4 tbsp chopped peanuts
3 tbsp sesame oil
500 ml (17 fl oz) Asian stock
3 tbsp peanut butter
200 g (7 oz) water chestnuts (tinned)
pepper

Minute 1
Peel and cube the shallots. Peel and finely chop the garlic.
Minute 4
Knead the shallots, garlic and egg yolk into the minced meat. Season with the soy sauce, five spice powder, salt and paprika.
Minute 8
Knead in the peanuts as well. Form the mix into small balls. Heat the oil in a fry pan and brown the meatballs on all sides for about 10 minutes, turning frequently.
Minute 18
Pour the stock into the pan and bring to the boil for a short time.
Minute 20
Stir the peanut butter into the stock. Drain and slice the water chestnuts, then stir them into the sauce as well. Season with salt and pepper.
Minute 23
Arrange everything on plates and serve with Asian noodles.

DESSERTS AND PUDDINGS

Just because you enjoy sweets does not mean that you have to "sin". Our seductive sweets are the crowning touch to any meal. And, naturally, they are all light and low in fat.

Desserts and puddings

ORANGE DESSERT

Preparation time: about 15 minutes
Serves 4

4 untreated oranges
300 g (10 oz) quark cheese (20 % fat)
50 g (2 oz) whole milk yoghurt
2 tbsp Triple Sec liqueur
100 ml (3 fl oz) orange juice
2 tbsp icing sugar
1 package vanilla sugar
80 g (2.75 oz) slivered almonds
1 tbsp sugar

Minute 1
Wash and dry the oranges. Use a zester to peel the orange rind in strips. Remove all the white skin with a sharp knife.

Minute 4
Fillet the orange pieces by cutting off the skin that separates the segments from each other. Put aside a few orange fillets for decoration. Purée the rest of the orange fillets with a handheld mixer.

Minute 9
Combine the quark and yoghurt, then stir in the Triple Sec, orange juice, icing sugar and vanilla sugar. Blend in the puréed fruit and half of the orange zest.

Minute 13
Toast the almonds in a pan with no fat. Sprinkle a little sugar over them.

Minute 15
Place some of the quark on each dessert plate, garnish with orange fillets, orange peel and slivered almonds. Serve.

RAINBOW FRUIT SALAD

Preparation time: about 20 minutes
Serves 4

2 pears
2 oranges
300 g (10 oz) strawberries
200 blue grapes
3 kiwifruits
lemon juice
3 tbsp brown sugar
1 tsp cinnamon
1 medium honeydew melon
mint for garnish

Minute 1
Rinse and pat dry the pears.
Halve them, remove seeds and
cut into thin wedges.

Minute 3
Peel the oranges, removing the
white skin. Separate orange
segments from the membrane.

Minute 5
Wash the strawberries and cut off
the stems. Rinse the grapes and
pat them dry. Halve them and
remove any seeds. Peel and slice
the kiwifruits.

Minute 10
Put the prepared fruit in a bowl
and drizzle lemon juice over it.
Stir the brown sugar and
cinnamon into the yoghurt.

Minute 14
Cut the top off the melon. Use
a melon baller to scoop out the
flesh of the melon and add to
the other ingredients.

Minute 19
Place the fruit salad in the melon
and top with the yoghurt. Garnish
with fresh mint and serve.

VANILLA RICE PUDDING

Preparation time: about 10 minutes
Serves 4

250 g (9 oz) five-minute rice
500 ml (17 oz) milk
6 tbsp currants
6 tbsp rose hip jam
250 ml (9 fl oz) vanilla sauce
(ready-made)
4 tbsp brown sugar
lemon balm for garnish

Minute 1
Boil the rice together with the milk, currants and rose hip jam for about 5 minutes.

Minute 7
Stir the vanilla sauce into the mixture and distribute amongst 4 dessert bowls.

Minute 10
Sprinkle each dish with brown sugar. Garnish with lemon balm and serve.

Minute 7

TIPSY PEARS

Preparation time: about 15 minutes
Serves 4

4 medium pears
4 tbsp lemon juice
500 ml (17 fl oz) dry red wine
250 ml (9 fl oz) port
1 sachet mulled wine spices
2 cinnamon sticks
5 tbsp honey
150 g (5 oz) goat cheese

Minute 1
Wash, peel and core the pears.
Score the pears several times
and drizzle with 2 tbsp of the
lemon juice.

Minute 4
Combine the red wine and port
in a pot. Add mulled wine spice
and cinnamon sticks and heat.

Minute 5
Add the remaining lemon juice
and honey. Let pears simmer in
this mixture for about 10 minutes
over low heat.

Minute 13
Cut the goat cheese in strips
and distribute on 4 dessert plates.
Remove the pears from the pot
and drain.

Minute 15
Lay pears on top of the cheese
and drizzle with the wine syrup.
Serve warm.

FANCY CREAM PUFFS

Preparation time: about 15 minutes
Serves 4

20 mini cream puffs (frozen)
250 g (9 oz) raspberries
200 g (7 oz) cream cheese
40 ml (1 fl oz) white raspberry brandy
1 tbsp sugar
3 tbsp cream
2 tbsp minced lemon balm
icing sugar to sprinkle
raspberries for garnish

Minute 1
Prepare cream puffs according to package instructions. Cut in half.

Minute 4
Rinse the raspberries and pat dry. Combine raspberries with the cream cheese, raspberry brandy, sugar, cream and lemon balm. Purée everything for a few moments with a handheld mixer.

Minute 11
Fill portions of the mixture into each cream puff and replace the lids. Dust with icing sugar and serve garnished with whole raspberries and lemon balm.

EGG-COCONUT SLICES

Preparation time: about 15 minutes
Serves 4

---

3 eggs
7 tbsp grated coconut
125 ml (4 fl oz) coconut milk
4 slices white bread
3 tbsp clarified butter
ground cinnamon
brown sugar

Minute 1
Whisk the eggs with the grated coconut and coconut milk.
Minute 3
Cut each bread slice in half and soak well in the egg mixture.
Minute 7
Heat clarified butter in a pan and fry slices on both sides for about 4 minutes.
Minute 15
Sprinkle with cinnamon and sugar. Serve warm.

Minute 1

Minute 3

Minute 7

Minute 15

PANCAKE STACKS

Preparation time: about 20 minutes
Serves 4

---

5 eggs
60 g (2 oz) wholegrain flour
60 g (2 oz) butter, softened
1 tsp ground aniseed
1 tsp ground cardamom
1 tsp orange peel or flavouring
1 pinch salt
500 ml (17 fl oz) milk
3 tbsp clarified butter
250 g (9 oz) red jam or preserves
250 g (9 oz) green jam or preserves
icing sugar for dusting

Minute 1
Beat the eggs with the flour and butter. Stir in the aniseed, cardamom, orange peel or flavouring and salt.
Minute 3
Stir in the milk and let stand for 5 minutes or so. Heat the clarified butter in a fry pan. Pour the batter into the pan in about 6 portions and cook until done.
Minute 15
Spread pancakes alternately with red and green jam and stack.
Minute 19
Cut the pancake stack into 4 pieces, dust with icing sugar and serve while still warm.

FRIED DATES

Preparation time: about 25 minutes
Serves 4

2 eggs
125 ml (4 oz) white wine
3 tbsp olive oil
2 tbsp sugar
100 g (3.5 oz) flour
salt
pepper
200 g (7 oz) cream cheese
4 tbsp lemon jelly
24 fresh dates
coconut oil for frying
lemon slices and lemon balm
for garnish

Minute 1
Beat the eggs with the wine, oil,
sugar and flour. Season lightly
with salt and pepper.

Minute 3
Combine the cream cheese and
lemon jelly. Cut the dates lengthwise and fill with the cream
cheese mixture.

Minute 10
Roll dates in the batter and then
fry in hot coconut oil until golden
brown.

Minute 24
Place the dates on lemon slices
and garnish with lemon balm.
Serve while warm.

INDEX OF RECIPES

A
Artichokes Lucullus, cooked 20
Asparagus on pappardelle 50
Avocado salad 18

B
Banana leaves, filled 85
Bistro roulades 102
Bratwurst salad 62

C
Caribbean sticks 101
Chicken livers in caper sauce 72
Coq au vin 58
Courgette ragout, exotic 21
Crabs on the shell 22
Crab-stuffed chicken 65
Crayfish, spicy 89
Cream puffs, fancy 115
Cream soup with crab meat 29

D
Dates, fried 118
Duck breast with fennel 66

E
Egg-coconut slices 116
Egg-flower broth with celery 35

F
Fish nuggets 82
Fish with tomato 77
Fruit salad, rainbow 112

G
Greek salad 19
Guinea fowl à l'orange 63

H
Halibut cocktail 22
Hare medallions 98

K
Kohlrabi gratin 54
Kohlrabi-thyme soup 33

L
Lamb chops with mango salsa 104
Lobster, baked 90

M
Macaroni "diabolo" 49
Meatballs, Asian 106
Meatballs, piquant 105
Mie goreng with prawns 76
Morel-olive pan 25
Moroccan soup 28
Mushroom fry-up, hearty 52
Mushroom soup with puff pastry top 30

N
Nasi rames 59
Noodle soup, colourful 38

O
Okra-mushroom soup 34
Orange dessert 110

P
Pancake stacks 116
Pea soup 36
Pears, tipsy 114
Penne with fennel cream 46
Perch dumplings 86
Perch-pike, braised 88
Pilaf, red garlic 47
Pita sandwiches 100
Plaice shish kebabs 80
Potato casserole 43
Poulard breasts, baked 73
Poultry curry, fruity 64
Poultry-herb risotto, quick 66

Q
Quail, fried 70
Quesadillas 42

R
Rice gratin, delicate 48
Rice stew 39
Rump steak with raita 98

S
Salmon gratin 90
Salmon shish kebabs 84
Savoy cabbage chops 96
Scampi cocktail Acapulco 14
Spanish vol-au-vents 54
Sprout-mushroom salad 16
Stew with ham 94
Sushi, chankin 15
Sushi, temaki 24
Sushi, temari 78

T
Teriyaki noodles 44
Tex-mex chilli 97
Thai drumsticks 68
Tomato soup 32
Tomato stew 36
Turbot rolls 81
Turkey roulades 60
Turkey steak & eggs 71

V
Vanilla rice pudding 113
Veal, poached 106
Vegetable shish kebabs, quick 53